need encouragement?

jason h. thomas

foreword by
pearilya l. thomas

Order this book online at www.trafford.com
or email orders@trafford.com

Most Trafford titles are also available at major online book retailers.

Note for Librarians: A cataloguing record for this book is available from Library
and Archives Canada at www.collectionscanada.ca/amicus/index-e.html

Printed in Victoria, BC, Canada.

ISBN: 978-1-4269-1399-0 (sc)

ISBN: 978-1-4269-1400-3 (dj)

Library of Congress Control Number: 2009933782

*We at Trafford believe that it is the responsibility of us all, as both individuals and corporations,
to make choices that are environmentally and socially sound. You, in turn, are supporting this
responsible conduct each time you purchase a Trafford book, or make use of our publishing services.
To find out how you are helping, please visit www.trafford.com/responsiblepublishing.html*

*Our mission is to efficiently provide the world's finest, most comprehensive book publishing
service, enabling every author to experience success. To find out how to publish your book, your
way, and have it available worldwide, visit us online at www.trafford.com*

Trafford rev. 8/20/2009

 www.trafford.com

North America & international
toll-free: 1 888 232 4444 (USA & Canada)
phone: 250 383 6864 ♦ fax: 250 383 6804 ♦ email: info@trafford.com

The United Kingdom & Europe
phone: +44 (0)1865 487 395 ♦ local rate: 0845 230 9601
facsimile: +44 (0)1865 481 507 ♦ email: info.uk@trafford.com

To those who have encouraged me and those who continue to encourage me, thank you.

Foreword

Have you ever awaken in the morning and said to yourself, "I need encouragement"? Do you know that God has given us the gift of encouragement? II Thessalonians 2: 16 & 17 says "May our Lord Jesus Christ himself and God our Father , who loved us and by His grace *gave us eternal encouragement* and good hope, encourage your hearts and strengthen you in every good deed and word." William Arthur Ward once said "Flatter me, and I may not believe you. Criticize me and I may not like you. Ignore me and I may not forgive you. Encourage me and I won't forget you."

Jason Thomas has been a dear husband, friend and most importantly a Barnabas (encourager) to me for a number of years. Being the wife of such a man of integrity fills my heart with glee. It is quite rewarding to have someone in your life that is dedicated to God and determined to fulfill His purposes.   He has a passion for the people and things of God. When it comes to encouraging God's people, Jason is unstoppable. His encouraging words and thoughts of the day have inspired thousands. He is a gifted writer, but more importantly through <u>need encouragement?</u>, he is an answer to someone's prayer.

As you take the time to read this book, know that it will serve as a source of daily encouragement for whatever situations that you may face. <u>need encouragement?</u> will strengthen you in your weak places, bring healing to your inner spirit, confirm things in which you may have been pondering, and give you hope to make it through another day.

As I have allowed the messages from this book to minister to me, I ask that you tune your hearts and minds in to what God has in store for you. The ultimate goal is to speak over yourself, encourage yourself, and then be able to get to a place where you can encourage others. Enjoy!

Opening Thoughts

The book that you hold in your hands possesses the power to revolutionize your life. You will laugh. You will be challenged in your thinking. You will examine the contents of your heart. You may even cry. But when all is said and done, you will be a better person because you took the time to read <u>need encouragement?</u>.

<u>need encouragement?</u> is a collection of thought-provoking, attitude-adjusting, and spirit-lifting writings intended to touch your heart and mind. As you read the following pages, I pray that you will open your heart, mind, and spirit to receive the things that you need. May you come away from reading this book excited, energized, and most importantly, encouraged.

Happy reading!

The Truth About Truth

Proverbs 27:6 tells us "Faithful are the wounds of a friend, but the kisses of an enemy are deceitful." I've heard it said that pain is inevitable, but misery is optional. In other words, while we must accept pain as a part of life, we don't have to let that pain define who we are. I know some people who wallow in self-pity and offense. They constantly maintain a "victim mentality" and their life motto seems to be "Woe is me!" Instead of allowing their wounds to make them better, they become bitter.

The greatest thing that a friend can do for you is to be honest, even when it hurts. While truth is confrontational and sometimes painful to hear, It is also liberating and refreshing. Truth helps move you from where you are to the place where God would have you to be. And while it is somewhat natural to recoil from the truth (especially the tough stuff), I encourage you to embrace truth. Truth brings health, healing, and wholeness. And what is this truth? Jesus tells us in John 17:17 "Sanctify them by Your truth. <u>Your word is truth</u>."

Make it your life goal and heart's desire to be a truth lover and a truth liver. Ye shall know the truth and the truth shall make you free!

Become What You Believe

You are just ONE decision away from becoming all that is abundantly in your heart! You alone are the one who can make that happen. It is my prayer that you will BECOME WHAT YOU BELIEVE! If you are believing for a better life, better relationships, better finances, better health, a better attitude, YOU have to make that decision. Your unbelief can hinder what God desires to do in your life.

If you are ready to make that decision to become what you believe, you need to focus on changing five things. You must change what you…

1. **<u>Say</u>**. You will have whatever you say (Mark 11:23).
2. **<u>See</u>**. You become whatever you behold. Whatever gains and sustains your attention will ultimately change your life.
3. **<u>Believe</u>**. All things are possible to those who believe (Matthew 19:26).

4. **<u>Think</u>**. As a man thinks in his heart, so is he (Proverbs 23:7).

5. **<u>Do</u>**. Be not only a hearer of the Word, but a doer also (James 1:22).

If you work on these five things, I believe that your life will go to another level and you will ultimately become what you believe.

You Get What You "Pray" For

The old cliché goes "You get what you pay for." I certainly believe this to be true with the quality of natural things. A cafeteria steak doesn't have quite the same taste as a steak from the finest steakhouse in the city. A used car with 100,000 miles doesn't run quite as smoothly as a brand new car fresh off the showroom floor. You tend to have more of a comfortable night's rest on 1000 count Egyptian sheets than the $9.99 sheets from Wal-Mart. In the natural, less expensive often means cheaper quality while more expensive often means higher quality.

In the spiritual realm, however, the quality of life is not based on what you **pay** for; it's about what you **pray** for. Jesus taught us that a man "will have whatever he says (Mark 11:23)." He also taught us that "whatever things you ask when you pray, believe that you receive them, and you will have them (Mark 11:24)." In other words, Jesus is telling us that "you get what you pray for." Now, does that mean that you'll get anything and everything that you pray for? Absolutely not! You will only get those things that are according to God's will for your life. And you come into an understanding of God's will for your life through prayer and understanding His Word.

If you are at a place in your life where you can't understand what's going on – you feel distant from God, your relationships are strained, your finances are in shambles, your health is declining, your career path is uncertain, your trust has been betrayed, or your attitude is negative – I encourage you to seek the Lord. Because He created you, He knows everything about you. He also wants nothing but the best for you (which is His good and acceptable and perfect will). So set aside some time to get into God's presence and allow Him to reveal His will for your life. Then, you will truly get what you pray for!

Spiritual Constipation

Have you ever experienced constipation? It's not the greatest feeling in the world, is it? You feel "clogged up" and irritable. With constipation, there is stuff going in you, but nothing is coming out. And when it does finally come out, one of two things happens:
1. It hurts or…
2. There is a sigh of relief.

The important thing is that it is out. The same can be said about "spiritual constipation". With spiritual constipation, you often feel "clogged up" if you don't allow things to come out of you that are bottled up. If God teaches you something or gives you insight into something, He doesn't intend for you to be the final destination. We often become "spiritually constipated" whenever we hold on to things that He intends for us to release. It could be an idea. It could be a compliment. It could be money. It could be your testimony. It could even be unforgiveness. Whatever it is, if it isn't released, it'll cause more harm than good.

Take the time to assess whether or not you are suffering from "spiritual constipation." Do you need to forgive someone? Do you need to share a comforting word with someone? Do you need to let your family know that you love them? Do you need to reconnect with a long lost relationship? Do you need to share your testimony? Do you need to return your tithe unto the Lord? Do you need to connect with a business partner? Where are you "clogged up"?

Make it a point to release whatever it is that needs to go. As Dr. Edwin Louis Cole taught, "You are taught to teach. You are blessed to bless. You are given to give. What God has done in you, for you, and to you, He now wants to do through you." So take a deep breath, take a spiritual laxative (inventory), and let "it" out!

The First...

When was the last time that you did something for the first time? Travelled to a place that you've never been? Learned something that you didn't know? Established a new relationship? Ate at a new restaurant? Attended a cultural event that is out of your comfort zone? Prayed for someone besides you and your immediate family?

Well, if it's been a while since your last "first", what are you waiting for? There is nothing that compares to experiencing "firsts". I will never forget the first time that I rode a roller coaster. I will never forget my first day of college. I will never forget the first time that I travelled outside of the United States. I will definitely never forget my first night as a married man. I will never forget watching my first child being born. I just love "firsts". It seems that you receive an extra dose of adrenalin whenever you experience "firsts".

When I turned 30 years old, priority, responsibility, and urgency began to take on new meaning for me. Maybe I've finally come to realize that life really IS short and I have to make the most of my time while I'm here. I don't want to approach the end of my life complaining of what I *coulda, woulda, shoulda.* Whenever it's my time to return to Jesus, I want to be confident that I've done everything that He desired of me as well as knowing that I had a great time while doing it.

I challenge you to take the time to ask yourself "What do I desire to do that I have yet to do? Where do I want to go that I haven't gone yet?" Once you answer these questions the final question to ask yourself is "What am I waiting on?"

I wish you the best as you experience your next "first".

Love...Love...Love

Ever been in love before? Puppy love? Go to the end of the earth love? I'll die for you love? Well, I'd like to bring a little clarity to this whole idea of love. I'd also like to define what love is and what it is not.

The definition of love that I often use is "an unconditional commitment to an imperfect person." When you truly love someone, there is nothing that can happen to remove or erase that love. He/she may mess up and make a number of mistakes, but your love for that person doesn't diminish. Love is an appreciating asset, not a depreciating liability. Love should always be based on who a person is and not what a person does. Also, love is not an emotion; it is a decision. Many couples choose to "call it quits" because they just don't "feel the love" anymore.

There are three primary areas where we must place our love. I John 4:8 tells us that "God is love." So, in an effort to share love with others, you are really sharing God with them. Focus on placing your love in the following areas:

1. **Love God**. Our relationship with God is the foundation for every relationship that we'll ever have. It is imperative that you have a proper relationship with God so that you can have proper relationships with others. God built us with a need to love Him. Be sure to love Him not merely in word or tongue but in deed and truth. In other words, don't just talk about it; be about it. Pray. Study your Bible. Pay your tithes. Serve in your church and community. Fellowship with other believers. These are all manifestations of your love for God.

2. **Love yourself**. You can only love others if you first love yourself. If you don't love yourself, you won't know how to relate to others. Take the time to love and affirm yourself. Make daily confessions

and affirmations regarding who God has created you to be. Remind yourself that you are fearfully and wonderfully made. Tell yourself that you are the apple of God's eye. Be confident in knowing that you're a King's kid.

3. **Love others**. The Bible tells us in John 13:35 "By this all will know that you are My disciples, if you have love for one another." When we have a proper and healthy love for God and ourselves, we then know how to love others. One of the most basic needs of all humanity is to be loved. What greater opportunity do we have than to serve as a source of love for someone else? Love is one of the few things that you can give to another person and never diminish your own supply. So take the time to love others.

The world needs a lot of things, but one of the greatest gifts that you have to offer is love. Why don't you take a moment right now to let someone know that you love them?

A Good N.A.M.E

Proverbs 22:1 states "A good name is to be chosen rather than great riches, loving favor rather than silver and gold."

If you desire to be a person who has a good N.A.M.E, you must have:

1. **"N"tegrity**.   In its simplest form, integrity means *always doing what's right.* I believe that a good name and integrity are inseparable. People who have a good name are those who have impeccable character and purity of heart. It doesn't mean that he/she never makes mistakes, but he/she is always quick to make things right whenever things do go wrong. So, the first element of having a good name is integrity.
2. **Attitude**. I'm a firm believer in the old adage that life is 10% what happens to you and 90% how you respond to it. People

who possess a positive attitude don't always have the best of everything, but they always make the best out of everything that they have. And it all starts with attitude. Having a positive attitude is a critical step in becoming a person with a good name. A positive attitude has a way of attracting positive things in your life. So take the time to focus on your attitude.

3. **Mastery**. A person with a good name is not a jack of all trades and a master of none. He/she has learned to master something. They give purposeful attention to areas of their strength. They develop their God-given gifts, talents, and abilities to bless the lives of others. While it is good to possess general knowledge on many topics, it is even better to have specific knowledge in particular areas. That is why a medical doctor who is a specialist makes more money than a general practitioner. Expertise is always better than general knowledge. So focus on mastering areas of your strength.

4. **Excellence**. Excellence simply means

doing the best that you can on the level where you are. Regardless of where you are in your life, you can be a person of excellence. People who desire to have a good name are people who strive for excellence in every area of life. They are not content with being ordinary, average, or mediocre. They are allergic to the status quo. People of excellence are always growing, always learning, always developing, always striving for something beyond where they currently are.

Ask yourself "What does my N.A.M.E say about me?" I hope and pray that you're satisfied with your answer. If not, take time to check your integrity, attitude, mastery, and excellence.

Are You T.O.U.G.H?

I've heard it said on numerous occasions that though tough times don't last, tough people do. And while I believe that to be true, I believe that tough times give us a great opportunity to grow through various situations.

In the midst of trying circumstances in my own life, it has caused me to examine myself and how I respond during those times. I've learned that tough times don't discriminate. It doesn't matter how saved or unsaved you are. It doesn't matter how old or young you are. It doesn't matter your race or ethnic background. It doesn't matter if you're a manager or an employee. It doesn't matter if you're single, married, divorced, or widowed. Tough times come to us all.

Being the optimist that I am, I try not to dwell on the details of the tough times but instead I aim to learn how I got into the tough situation, the lessons that I am to learn from the situation, and steps I need to take to get out of it.

As you experience tough times in your life, I encourage you to respond by being a T.O.U.G.H person:

Transparent. People can't be helped until they're willing to be transparent. The more a person hides, the less they desire to be helped. But once a person opens themselves up, the possibilities are endless.

Obedient. If we truly believe God and His Word, we can be confident that our obedience will benefit us much better than our own reasoning. It is often our disobedience or disbelief that throws us off the course that God has set for us.

Understanding. I strive to live my life as a person who seeks to understand more so than to be understood. Seeking to understand builds a bond with others that can't be established any other way. As we seek to understand the hearts and minds of others, we often understand more about ourselves in the process.

Grateful. Gratitude is a way to ensure that more comes into your life. And I'm not merely referring to material things. I'm speaking of being grateful for things like love, grace, peace, joy, family, and healing. Great people are grateful people.

Humble. In addition to being grateful, the greatest people I've ever met have also been extremely humble. Humility is not thinking less of yourself but simply thinking of yourself less. The Bible reminds us in James 4:6 that "God resists the proud, but gives grace to the humble." Do what's necessary to be a recipient of His grace.

Satisfaction

What is the primary source of your satisfaction? Performing well at work? Having peace and harmony at home? Having money in your bank account? Being a blessing to someone else? Maintaining a healthy body?

Take the time to examine what satisfaction means and looks like to you. It means a variety of things to people, so it's important that you take the time to define what satisfaction looks like to *you*. Don't allow anyone else to define it for you. Whenever you allow someone else to create your world for you, they'll always create it too small.

Whatever your definition is of satisfaction, allow God to satisfy you in only a way that He can. He is the source of ALL joy, peace, understanding, wisdom, patience, compassion, and love. May He fill you in every place that you're lacking and may He remove things and people that might be hindering you from obtaining all that He has for you!

The Purpose of Pain

Have you ever felt as if your pain was perpetual and your wound incurable? Have you ever hurt so bad that you didn't know how you would go on? Have you ever wrestled with your emotions to the point where you couldn't sleep well at night? Has your heart and mind ever been at war and you didn't know which one was right? If you have, you are definitely not alone.

In the midst of your pain and despair, never lose hope. Although it may hurt and your next step may not seem clear, continue to trust God. I know that's not the answer that most folks want to hear when they're going through difficulties, but it honestly is the best remedy. You might have to trust God while you are kicking, screaming, and cussing on the inside, but continue to trust Him nonetheless.

Although I am acquainted with pain more than I care to acknowledge, my perspective on pain has been shaped and molded due to various experiences that I have had. I have come to accept the fact that while pain is inevitable, misery is optional. I have also learned that pain is nothing more than weakness leaving and strength developing. My prayer is that you won't simply allow yourself to feel pain but grow through it. I also pray that you will willingly usher weakness out of your life and welcome strength with open arms. Don't always fight the pain in your life! It comes to serve a purpose. As you continue to seek God, He will give you clarity as to exactly what that purpose is.

Fill Your Heart

Our hearts have a certain capacity level, both naturally and spiritually. It is up to us to decide what takes root in our hearts. And based on our "diet" and decisions, the contents of our hearts are determined. The more that we fill our hearts with good, healthy, and productive things, our lives will gravitate towards growth, progress, and development. However, if our hearts are constantly exposed to negativity, small mindedness, and dream killers, our lives will remain stagnant or even grow worse.

Today, make a decision to fill your heart with...

- A greater understanding of who God is
- A greater comprehension of His love towards you
- A greater understanding of who He has made YOU to be
- A hunger to know more

- A greater level of compassion towards others
- A commitment to make a difference in the life of someone else

It's not ironic that Solomon told us to "Guard your heart with all diligence, for out of it spring the issues of life (Proverbs 4:23)." Stay on guard!

Through It All...

One morning, I clearly heard the Lord say to me "Through it all." When He said it, I honestly didn't fully comprehend what He meant. After spending more time in His presence, I believe that He would have me to remind you that He is with you through it ALL. Despite how bad things may seem right now, He is with you. No matter how dysfunctional your relationships may be, God is with you. No matter how messed up your financial situation might be right now, God is with you. Even though your dreams aren't panning out the way you thought they would and are beginning to seem more like fantasies, God is with you. Even if you are not fully satisfied with your current place of employment, God is with you.

During times of depression and discouragement, God is with you. During times of confusion and fatigue, God is with you. In successes and failures, He is with you. In times of clarity and times of cloudiness, He is right there with you. In lack and in plenty, God is there. In sickness and divine health, He is with you. Even in belief or disbelief, God is with you through it ALL.

Never doubt in the light those things that He spoke to you while you were in the dark. He is faithful. He is stable. And He is with you through it all.

Alone With Your Thoughts

In Tyler Perry's movie "The Family That Preys", Kathy Bates' character tells her son, "It's not you that I don't trust. It's your personal thoughts!" What a true statement! Often times, it is the innermost thoughts and desires of a person that ultimately leads them to trouble. That is why we must take extra caution to guard our thoughts.

The apostle Paul provides us with direction on how to focus our thoughts in the book of Philippians. "Finally, brethren, whatever things are true, whatever things are noble, whatever things are just, whatever things are pure, whatever things are lovely, whatever things are of good report, if there is any virtue and if there is anything praiseworthy – meditate on these things (Phil. 4:8)."

My favorite time of day is between 2:00 am and 6:00 am. Maybe it's just me, but that's the best time to think, meditate, and pray. It's during that time frame that it seems as if the entire world is asleep and I am the only one who is awake. Thoughts seem clearer and prayers seem unhindered during those times. There is a freshness and peace that can't be found during other times of the day.

At times when you find yourself alone with your thoughts, take Paul's advice and meditate on true, noble, just, pure, lovely, virtuous, praiseworthy things that are of good report. Don't be afraid of being alone with your thoughts. Instead, relish those times and allow God to restore your soul (mind, will, intellect, and emotions).

Burned, Washed, Blown

Have you ever struggled with something that just won't seem to go away? Excess weight? A bad attitude? A nagging health problem? Ungodly thoughts? A secret sin? Impure desires in your heart? Better yet, have you ever dealt with *someone* who won't go away? I won't go there!

There are three primary ways that things are removed from our lives:

1. **Burned**. Have you ever been "burned" by a person or situation before? God sometimes has to allow you to be burned by a person or experience in order to get it out of your life. And although the heat may burn you, you will eventually heal. Fire is also used to purify things. During times when things are being burned out of your life, realize that God is also removing impurities that don't belong. Sometimes,

we have to be consumed by His fire so that we won't be consumed by the wrong types of things.

2. **Washed**. Things are bound to get dirty in our lives. Our houses. Our cars. Our offices. Even our mindsets and attitudes can get dirty from time to time. It sometimes takes pure and clean things to overtake our lives and remove all the "dirt". Once we've been "burned", we can then immerse ourselves in "water" to be washed. Water is another way that God cleanses and purifies us. The best "water" we can depend on to cleanse us is the Word of God.

3. **Blown**. The things that remain after you've been burned and washed can be blown away. What is not consumed by fire nor washed by water can be blown by the wind of the Spirit. The wind comes to move things that couldn't be reached by fire or water. Often times, the winds that come are the words that are spoken from our mouths or the mouths of others. Words possess the power to build up or

tear down, to bless or curse, to produce life or produce death. Guard your words.

Whether you have to deal with fire, water, or wind, be confident that God is with you no matter what. He is the One who is able to help you weather the storms of life.

Are You Content
With Your Contents?

Are you content with yourself?
Not with your job…
Not with your bank account…
Not with your wardrobe…
Not with your relationships…
Not with your car…
Not with your investment portfolio (or lack thereof)…
Simply with yourself.

Are you happy with the person that God has made you to be? Contentment is always based on your contents – what's on the inside of you.

Have you discovered what all lies inside of you?
Have you discovered the treasure that you are?

Have you discovered that you are a blessing in the lives of others?

Have you discovered that you have multiple gifts and talents?

Have you discovered that you have a unique calling and purpose for being on the Earth?

Have you discovered that you are beautiful?

Have you discovered that you are a person of excellence because you are a child of a King?

Have you discovered that you are destined for greatness?

Have you discovered that someone needs you?

Have you discovered that you are blessed beyond measure?

If not, what are you waiting on?

Discovering peace and contentment is always an "inside job." So take the time to do some self-examination and discover all that lies on the inside of you. The world desperately needs your contents.

Frustration Management

Do you currently find yourself in a state of frustration? Frustrated with your job? Frustrated with your spouse? Frustrated with your children? Frustrated with your financial situation? Frustrated with your health? Frustrated with your creditors? Frustrated with what your life has become?

Well, join the club. Frustration is something that we'll all encounter at some point or another. The real test is how you respond to the frustration that you experience in your life. Do you bottle it up and not talk about the things that frustrate you? Do you snap at the first sign of frustration in your life? Do you mistreat others close to you as a result of being frustrated? Do you resort to alcohol or drugs to soothe your pain? Or do you have a healthy response? What is your answer to frustration when it comes into your life? Allow me to offer some "food for thought" when you experience frustration.

Change your activities and do something to relax so that you can renew your perspective. You need a break, a diversion, something to relax you where you don't give serious thought to things you may be facing. Once you are refreshed, life takes on a whole different meaning and perspective. When you are tired and frustrated, you need a break to enter into rest. You need a change of scenery and thoughts. You have to create fresh memories and rejuvenate your spirit. Do something fun that won't cause you stress. Laugh. Travel. Read. Exercise. Pray. Volunteer. Pull back in some areas and allow yourself to have renewed energy, focus, and perspective.

Don't allow frustration to get the best of you! It's all about how you respond to it as it comes your way. You are well equipped! Don't be frustrated; become rejuvenated!

Be The One

In the midst of everything going on in today's world, it's imperative that men and women begin to arise and cry out on behalf of the lost, the last, and the least. We have arrived at a period of time where we must pray like never before. We must seek the heart of God like never before. We must discern the voice of the Lord like never before. We must live according to godly principles like never before. We must abide by our convictions like never before. We must be willing to stand up for what is right like never before. We must be willing to listen to the content of people's hearts like never before. We must discover our calling and operate in it like never before. We must be willing to serve the needs of others like never before. We must fight the devil like never before. We must protect our families like never before. We must dream bigger dreams and set loftier goals like never before. We must be willing to risk what others won't and do what others don't. We must believe for miracles like never before. We must work towards restoration like never before. We must believe for healing like never before.

One day at a time, trusting God one step at a time, living beyond yourself, you can be the one that the world is searching for.

Be the one to stop:
- Alcoholism
- Drug addiction
- Low self-esteem
- Financial mismanagement
- Ignorance
- Anger
- Racism
- Sexism
- Mediocrity
- Having children out of wedlock
- Health challenges
- Mental illness
- Adultery
- Divorce
- Lack of faith
- Bad parenting

- Lack of moral integrity
- Physical and emotional abuse

In the words of Gandhi, "We must be the change that we desire to see in the world."

Make a decision today to be the one that the world needs.

The Blessing of Relationship

It's amazing how your life can either move forward or revert backwards simply based on the relationships that are in your life. Three wonderful "people principles" have been engrained in my heart:

1. God's answer to every problem is always a person (the right person in the right place at the right time doing the right thing).
2. People are like elevator buttons – they take you up, down, or get you stuck.
3. Those closest to you will determine your level of success.

Your life will never get to the level where it should be until you have the proper people in the proper positions in your life. Remember that proper people placement prevents problems. As Dr. John Maxwell says, "It's not about having everyone on the bus. It's about making sure that everyone is in their proper seat on the bus."

Every relationship in your life should serve a purpose. If it serves no purpose, it is important to eliminate that relationship from your life. It is unhealthy to carry "excess baggage". There are times when there may be someone in your life who is not meant to be there. And in the process of them being there, they are blocking you from receiving a wonderful relationship that God intends for you to have.

Take the time to evaluate the relationships in your life. Are they helping you to grow or are they stunting your growth? Can you be yourself and still be unconditionally loved? Proverbs 27:6 says "Wounds from a sincere friend are better than many kisses from an enemy." In any relationship, disagreements and misunderstandings are bound to happen. However, don't allow those things to destroy the God-ordained relationships in your life. Those disagreements and misunderstandings should only draw you closer together.

Value the relationships that God has blessed

you with. God has called us to value people and use things, not to use people and value things. Relationships are a gift from God. Never forget that! Now, take the time to call, email, or write someone and let them know how much they mean to you.

Time of Transition

We are in a time of great transition. The seasons are changing. Leadership is changing. Relationships are changing. The political landscape is changing. Educational policies are changing. The stock market is changing. Ministry methodologies are changing. The housing market is changing. Sports records are changing. Everywhere you look, there is change.

Don't be afraid of change. Learn to embrace it. Change, however, should not be your ultimate goal. Instead, you should strive to grow. Growth is really nothing more than sustained change. Growth is a tremendous asset because it does several things for us.

1. Growth prepares us to receive things on a greater level than where we currently are.
2. Growth affords us the opportunity to develop relationships that enhance and

maximize our gifts and talents.

3. Growth enables us to establish and maintain a greater level of influence with others.

During this time of transition, I encourage you to do the following:

1. **Trust God**. Even when you don't understand what is going on in your life, you must trust that He has your best interest at heart.

2. **Maintain your flexibility**. You must remain pliable in the Master's hand. Don't get stuck in one particular way of anything. God is sovereign and can do anything He wants to do, whenever He wants to do it, in any way that He wants to do it, through any person that He chooses to do it.

3. **Keep your eyes, ears, and heart open**. Opportunities are all around you. You must remain sensitive and discerning to what God intends for your life.

4. **Journal**. Chronicle all of the wonderful lessons that you are learning during this

time. This will not only bless you but it will bless your children as well as others with whom you have influence.

5. **Enjoy the journey**. Let your hair down and learn to laugh often. Jesus came that we might have life and have it more abundantly (John 10:10).

This is an exciting time to be alive! Always remember that change is inevitable, but growth is optional. So, grow well!

The Problem With Problems

Ever encountered a problem in your life? Stress in your relationships? A challenge with your finances? Difficulty on your job? Not enough money for gas?

If so, don't fret! Problems are a normal part of life. Don't get discouraged when you encounter problems. Too many people believe that a problem has to be a problem. And it doesn't have to be. You can prepare yourself in advance so that you can respond properly to your problems.

Allow me to share a quote with you that provides a wonderful perspective on problems:

"Understand that most problems are a good sign. Problems indicate that progress is being made, wheels are turning, you are moving toward your goals. Beware when you have no problems. Then

you've really got a problem. Problems are like landmarks of progress." ~ Scott Alexander

Although you'll encounter problems from time to time, let them serve as catalysts to help propel you towards your goals. Your progress may not always seem evident at the time, but your problems are ultimately working for your greater good. Believe that!

So, do you still view your problem as a problem?

Birth Pains

Have you ever encountered resistance whenever you try to accomplish your goals and fulfill your dreams? Have you ever found it difficult to bring to completion something that is abundantly in your heart? Have you ever wanted to give up on doing something that is a passion of your heart?

If so, you are certainly not alone. As a matter of fact, you are normal for experiencing those types of emotions. Whenever you have your heart set on accomplishing anything of significance, it is inevitable that you will experience pain and resistance. But those things are normal to the birthing process. Even in the natural, whenever a woman is birthing a child into the world, there is a tremendous amount of pain associated with it. However, once the child arrives, the pain that was felt just a few moments earlier dissipates and immediately turns into joy. The pain of the experience is quickly forgotten and replaced with joy.

Maintain the proper perspective as you pursue your goals, dreams, and aspirations. Realize that pain is a part of the process, but don't allow that to hinder you from going after those things. Anything that is made must go through process. You will be a better person because of it. As Paul said in Hebrews 12:1-2, "Let us run with endurance the race that is set before us, looking unto Jesus, the author and finisher of our faith…" Keep your eyes upon Him, allow Jesus to be your anchor and He will certainly help you to bring your goals, dreams, and aspirations to pass.

The Three C's

If you ever hope to be successful in life, you have to intentionally act upon certain principles. Living your life according to principle will alleviate the stress of making certain decisions. In other words, whenever you live your life according to principle, 99% of your decisions are already made.

Allow me to share three principles with you that will ensure your success in life.

1. **<u>Don't compare</u>**. Never compare yourself with anyone else. Two things happen as a result of comparisons. If you compare yourself to someone on a lower level or in a worse situation than you, you develop a certain sense of arrogance. On the flip side, if you compare yourself to someone on a higher level or in a better situation, you will develop an inferiority complex. Neither of these is healthy. Only compare

yourself to yourself, your purpose, your destiny, and your abilities.

2. **<u>Don't compete</u>**. God only expects of you the things that He knows that **<u>you're</u>** capable of. Everyone isn't gifted to sing or speak or write well. However, God has given every person a unique ability. And He expects you to use it for His glory. Take your eyes off of what someone has and begin to look at what God has placed on the inside of you. It's more there than you can imagine.

3. **<u>Don't complain</u>**. There are many things that you could complain about, but try not to. Whenever you feel the urge to complain about something, find something that you can speak positively about instead. Complaining keeps you connected to your problems. The more you complain, the more you keep yourself bound to whatever is affecting you. Begin to replace your complaints, gripes, and mealy mouthing with positive thoughts, compliments, and praise.

If you will implement these three simple principles, you will begin to "c" a world of difference.

The Opinions That Matter

I am a firm believer that people have a greater need to be reminded than they do to be informed. Based on that principle, this writing is intended to remind some while inform others about the three opinions that *ultimately* matter in life:

1. God's opinion of you.
2. Your opinion of God.
3. Your opinion of yourself.

Often times, we make the mistake of focusing more on the opinions of people than we do on God's opinion of us or even our opinion of ourselves. That is a terrible mistake to make. While it is "nice" for people to have a favorable opinion of us, our ultimate focus should be to ensure that God is pleased with us and that we are happy with ourselves. Take the time to ask yourself:

- How does God feel about me?
- How do I feel about God?
- How do I feel about myself?

In a nutshell, God has an extremely favorable opinion of you. Jeremiah 29:11 says "I know the plans that I have for you, declares the Lord. Plans to prosper you and not to harm you; plans to give you hope and a future." God has your best interest at heart! God desires for you to prosper and be in good health! God desires for your family to be healthy and whole. God is confident in your gifts, talents, and abilities because He is the One who blessed you with them! God loves you more than you can imagine! Even in spite of your faults and failures, God loves you! You are the apple of His eye and His most precious creation!

And just how do you see yourself? Well, if you believe that you are truly made in God's image and after His likeness, you ought to feel pretty good about yourself (not in an arrogant or conceited manner). If, for some reason, you have lost focus or are unsure of yourself, commit time to reading His Word and see what your Father has to say about you.

Don't Wait

Have you ever had a root canal performed before? If you've ever had one done, you know that it's not the most pleasant experience in the world. However, it's necessary if you don't want your mouth to be permanently messed up. At one time, I had to have a root canal performed. Now here's the amazing thing. I had known for quite some time that I needed to have this procedure done. But I kept putting it off and putting it off and putting it off until I finally couldn't bear the pain any longer. I literally woke up one night in tears because my mouth was in so much pain. Reflecting on this whole experience, it's amazing how the smallest things, when they go unattended, can cause the greatest problems.

While I was having my mouth operated on, I began to think about what God desired for me to learn through this experience. And here is the lesson that I learned: The longer you neglect certain things in your life, the more expensive, time-consuming, and painful it becomes when you do choose to address it.

Here is my question to you: What have you been putting off? Here is a list of questions to ask yourself if you feel like you've been "slow" in dealing with certain things in your life:

- Do I need to give my heart FULLY to the Lord?
- Do I need to forgive someone who has hurt or offended me?
- Do I need to believe for greater things on a higher level than where I currently am?
- Do I need to make some beneficial changes for my body (more exercise, better eating habits, getting adequate rest, drinking more water, cutting down on eating sweets, eating more fresh fruits and vegetables, etc.)?
- Do I need to start living on a budget and stop all of my wasteful, frivolous spending?
- Do I need to tell someone that I love them

and appreciate them for who they are in my life?

- Do I need to take the time to write my vision?
- Do I need to remove someone from my life who means me no good?
- Do I need to give more time to the Lord and my family and less time to my job?
- Do I need to move from in front of the TV or computer and pick up a book?
- Do I need to turn off the radio and iPod and begin to talk to God?

Whatever it is, don't wait. Make the necessary changes in your life that you KNOW you need to make. Time is of the essence. There are people who are connected to your life that need what you have to offer. So don't wait another minute. Do what you need to do today!

What's Really Important?

Ever feel as if your work is in vain? Ever feel that whenever you take two steps forward that you take three back? Ever feel as if you always have to start back at square one? Ever feel overworked and underappreciated?

Never lose focus of the purpose of everything that you do. The Bible tells us in Colossians 3:23 that "whatever you do, do it heartily, as to the Lord and not to men." God is the One who will provide you with your reward. Too often, we look for people to give us the assurance and confidence that only God can give. Proverbs 3:26 teaches that "For the Lord will be your confidence." Always remember that God is your Creator. He is the One who knows everything about you. Any question that you have can be answered by seeking Him and His Word.

While I realize that there is a lot going on in the world today and a lot of things to distract your attention, I pray that you never lose focus on what's truly important – faith, family, love, legacy, purpose, destiny. Whenever you feel overwhelmed and overextended, be sure to not merely prioritize your schedule but learn to schedule your priorities. God's depending on you!

Halftime

I am an avid sports fan. My wife might even call me a football addict. We all have our vices, don't we?☺ But one of the best parts of football (or even basketball) is halftime. This is a time where you have already played two quarters and you still have two left. Teams have implemented their initial strategy and plan and now they have time to sit, think, regroup, and re-strategize. Time to evaluate what they've done, make the necessary adjustments, and hopefully improve their performance in the second half.

The two greatest things that you can engage during the "halftimes" of your life are:

1. The creative power of your mind
2. The power of collective thinking and perspective

As you prepare for the "second halves" of your life, I encourage you to utilize the power of your mind as well as the perspective and counsel of others close to you. Devote dedicated time to evaluate where you are in your life (not where you think you are). Be willing to ask yourself the tough questions and answer them truthfully. What goals did you set out to work on? How is your progress coming on accomplishing them? Is your motivation to finish them strong enough? What changes do you need to make in order to finish what you started? Engage your mind and determine where you currently are and what you'd like your life to look like from this point forward.

Ask counsel of other people who have your best interests at heart. There are some haters in this world, so be careful who you seek advice from. Spend time with people who are already where you want to be. Stop running with people on your level and start running with people on the level that you aspire to be. I will be the first to admit that it is uncomfortable to grow and change, but at the end of the day, you're a better person for it. So take advantage of the relationships that are in your life. Ask questions. Take notes. Initiate dialogue. Act on the wisdom that others share with you.

Time waits for no one. You better get to work. Halftime is over and it's time for the "second half".

Triple A

There are three basic needs of every human being. And I am not talking about food, clothing, and shelter. While those are certainly important to our livelihood, the three basic needs that I'm speaking of are:

1. Attention
2. Affection
3. Appreciation

1. **<u>Attention</u>**.   Every human being, regardless of age, race, faith, or political affiliation, has a need for attention. They need to know that someone notices that they exist, that they matter. One of the greatest benefits about attention is that it doesn't even cost you anything to give it to someone, at least not financially. All it requires of you is your time and your devotion to look beyond yourself.

Attention is the first need of every human being.

2. **Affection**. Who doesn't appreciate a little TLC? A hug, a smile, a pat on the back, a playful bump, a held hand, a kiss. We all have a need for affection. Whenever I leave my house, I make it a point to hug and kiss my wife and children because I realize just how important affection is. I make it a point to show affection as a means of connecting with others. If it's a pat on the shoulder or a hug, it's important to show affection to others. Affection often helps to relieve stress in people. Studies have been done that show the healing power of a gesture of affection.

3. **Appreciation**. Everyone desires to be appreciated. Appreciation, like attention, doesn't cost anything except your time and a selfless attitude. People want to know that what they do matters. They want to know that they are making a difference. A simple "thank you" or "I appreciate you" may mean more to someone than

you may realize. So strive to live your life with gratitude and appreciation.

Take the time to give someone your undivided attention, unexpected affection, and unconditional appreciation. They'll be blessed by it and so will you.

You're The Answer

In today's world, there are many opportunities for you to be a blessing to others. The primary way that you can be a blessing and make an impact in the world is to become a problem solver and solution provider. The greatest way to become invaluable is to become an answer to a problem. The truth of the matter is that there will always be problems, however, it takes a person of excellence to provide a solution. The average person will take a look around and say "What is this world coming to?" The excellent person will examine things and say "What can I do to help eliminate poverty? How can I serve as a resource to a young person who doesn't have a father at home? What's the best way to offer hope to those who are discouraged? What can I do to make the road easier for those who are coming behind me? Is there an organization or business that I can establish that will create opportunities for others? How can I keep others from making the same mistakes that I've made? What's my responsibility to my family and my household? What can I do to restore values and morals to society?" There are a number of questions that need to be answered…and YOU are the answer!

It's one thing to pray and seek God for an answer, but it's another thing to become an answer. Please know that God's answer to every problem is always a person. Money isn't always the answer to problems because money doesn't solve every problem. Ecclesiastes 10:19 says "But money answers everything." In the proper context, that verse means that money answers all money-related issues. However, God's answer to every problem is always a person. God will always send the right person to the right place at the right time to do the right thing. Problems tend to arise when the wrong person is in the wrong place at the wrong time doing the wrong thing.

During a time of imprisonment and slavery, God didn't attempt to draft up some type of emancipation proclamation. Instead, He raised up a person, Moses, to serve as a deliverer of His people. When the walls of Jerusalem were broken down and laid in ruins, God didn't organize a construction company nor did He seek to hire a general contractor. He raised up a person, Nehemiah, to rebuild those broken down walls. When the world was full of sin and contumacy, God didn't perform mass genocide and take everyone out because of their sin. He sent His son, Jesus, to die for our sins and become the Savior of the world.

What problem has God placed you in the Earth to solve? Where does your passion lie? What ignites your heart? Marriage and family? Health and fitness? Finances? Business? Counseling? Writing? Dancing? Singing? Cooking? Teaching? Cleaning? If you are uncertain as to where you passion lies, here are four questions to ask yourself to gain clarity:

1. What do I dream about?
2. What do I cry about?
3. What makes me happy?

4. What breaks/burdens my heart?

Wherever your passion lies, give your all to it. God's counting on you! Now, be all that He's made you to be!

What Do You V.A.L.U.E?

Values serve as safeguards and boundaries for your life. Your core values are the deeply held beliefs that authentically describe your soul. Your values are the very essence of who you are. It's been said that "Methods are many, values are few. Methods often change, values never do." So exactly what is V.A.L.U.E?

Virtue. Webster defines virtue as "conformity to a standard of right; morality; a commendably quality or trait." You should strive to live your life so that you are judged by the wealth of your virtue and not the virtue of your wealth. Being a virtuous man or woman is an essential ingredient of being a person of V.A.L.U.E.

Ability. Your value can also be determined by the abilities that you possess. In other words, what you have to offer. What are your natural gifts, talents, and abilities? Your goal should be to utilize your ability to add value to the lives of others.

Love.   Love is defined as an unconditional commitment to an imperfect person.   God realized the importance of love so much so that He summed up all the commandments and law into two:

1. Love the Lord with all your heart, mind, soul, and strength.
2. Love your neighbor as yourself.

Understanding.   A famous person once said that "We should strive to understand first; then strive to be understood." That is a true statement if I've ever heard one!   Our goal should be to understand God first, ourselves second, and others third.

Excellence.   Excellence is doing the best you can on the level where you are.   Also, it is true that you will only excel at what you do well. Strive to let excellence, not perfection, be your goal.   Daniel was a young man who had an excellent spirit in him. That should be our goal as well.

As you focus on Virtue, Ability, Love, Understanding, and Excellence, you will be well on your way to becoming a person of **V.A.L.U.E.**

The Power of Two: Double Blessing or Double Trouble?

"Two are better than one; because they have a good reward for their labor. For if they fall, the one will lift up his fellow; but woe to him that is alone when he falleth; for he hath not another to help him up. Again, if two lie together, then they have heat; but how can one be warm alone? And if one prevails against him, two shall withstand him; and a threefold cord is not quickly broken." ~ Ecclesiastes 4:9-12

"And he called unto him the twelve, and began to send them forth by *two and two...*" ~ Mark 6:7

Think of all the great duos that have ever existed...

Batman and Robin...

Magic and Kareem...

Big Boi and Andre 3000 (my personal favorite)…
Tom and Jerry…
Heathcliff and Claire Huxtable (a close second)…

Now think of the "not so great" duos…
Ike and Tina…
Bobby and Whitney…
Elizabeth Taylor and her previous 8 husbands…

With any of these duos, each person needed the other one to become who they were supposed to be. They each provided something. In any relationship, there should always be some sense of mutuality.

Who's your main partner? Are they an asset or a liability to you? Are they a blessing or a curse? There is a tremendous power in partnership, but you want to make sure that you have the right partner with you. You want someone who helps you to grow and not merely someone who keeps you on the same level where you are. You ought to have people close to you that challenge you. At the same time, you want people who affirm you and understand and support your destiny and calling. You want people who will encourage you and believe the best in you. Your main partner should be someone with whom you can be both accountable and vulnerable. They should be able to see the preciousness of who you are and be willing and able to overlook your flaws and idiosyncrasies.

Don't minimize the power of partnership. The people closest to you will determine the direction of your life. It is true that birds of a feather not only flock together, but they also fly to the same destination. Even in scripture, we see that people understood the benefit and blessing of partnership. Moses had Joshua. David had Jonathan. Elijah had Elisha. Paul had Timothy. Jesus had Peter, James, and John. If these guys needed partners, we are certainly no different.

Take inventory of who's "on your team". You will probably need to cut some folks off. Other folks need to be "redirected" to another team. You have to ensure that you have proper "cap space" to make room for the people that are destined to be with you. You don't want anyone with you who's not meant to be with you.

Having the right people on your team makes the journey much more enjoyable and worthwhile. So check your relationships and walk in your "double blessing"!

Sovereign

Webster defines sovereign as "superlative in quality; excellent; of the most exalted kind; supreme; of an unqualified nature; having undisputed ascendancy; paramount; unlimited in extent; absolute; enjoying autonomy; independent."

Sovereign is certainly an adjective that accurately describes the very essence of who God is. The God that I love and serve is truly sovereign. To paraphrase Brother Webster's definition, "God can do what He wants to do, when He wants to do it, and how He wants to do it. He knows all, sees all, and controls all." At times, it is overwhelming to imagine the sovereignty of our God. However, it ought to serve as a source of comfort to know that God is truly the controller of the universe. In spite of the chaotic circumstances that are currently in our world (terrorism, war, school shootings, divorce, random violence, downsizing, foreclosures, etc.), you can rest assured that God is still sitting on His throne and has things under control, even the everyday affairs of your life.

If you have lost a loved one, God is still in control. If your marriage is on the rocks, God is still in control. If your children are acting in a way that you didn't raise them, God is still in control. If you are having a few financial setbacks (or a lot of financial issues), God is still in control. If you can't see the end of your troubles and don't know how things could ever get better, know that God is still in control. If your job or school is stressing you out, know that God is still in control. If it seems as if you have false friends and real enemies, God is still in control. If you seem to take two steps forward and five steps back, God is still in control. It doesn't matter where you currently are. God is large enough to meet you right where you are. He loves you too much to allow you to stay where you are! God is progressive and not recessive! Philippians 3:13 exhorts us to "forget those things which are behind (failures, mistakes, things we have no power to change) and reach forward to those things which are ahead (goals, dreams, God-given purpose, the fulfillment of our calling)."

If you are discouraged and have grown weary in your well doing, I simply want to remind you that God is truly sovereign. He knows what you're going through and He is committed to helping you achieve everything that He has in store for you. Don't faint! Don't grow weary! Don't lose heart! You're closer to your destiny than you've ever been! Keep pressing forward! You will obtain what you are seeking if you refuse to give up.

Speech or Silence?

Have you ever been faced with a decision as to whether you ought to "speak your peace" or keep silent? Have you ever been so disturbed by what's going on in the world that you know that you MUST do something about it? Have you ever been offended by someone so badly that verbal or physical retaliation seems like the only viable solution? If so, read on.

Dr. Edwin Louis Cole once said "A man's silence lets the devil shout. When Christians speak, the devil is silent." During times when you don't know whether to speak or keep silent, be mindful that there are only three people that you should speak to:

1. **God**. I Peter 5:7 tells us to "cast all your care upon Him, for He cares for you." Because God truly has your best interest at heart, it is best to go to Him FIRST. As you talk to Him, He'll work things out

on your behalf. He is truly a confidante and place of refuge. So speak to God, not only in times when you're in trouble but each and every day.

2. **Yourself**. I Samuel 30:6 says that "David encouraged himself in the Lord." You sometimes have to speak to yourself. I don't mean this in a "crazy" way, but you have to become your own cheerleader at times. You have to speak health and healing when you may feel like death is inevitable. You have to speak peace and joy when you are depressed and suicidal. Words truly have creative power, so begin to speak things to yourself. The Bible tells us that a thing decreed shall be established. So begin to declare things by faith. If you don't like the way that things are going in your life, begin to speak those things that be not as though they already were.

3. **Others**. James 5:16 says "Confess your trespasses to one another, and pray for one another, that you may be healed." Before you open your mouth and heart to another human being, PLEASE be sure that you

can trust them. There's nothing worse than sharing your secrets with an enemy. Trust is extended to the limit of truth and no further. You have to know who's really "for you". Despite what you may believe, everyone is not really "on your side". Everyone is not happy to see you prosper and progress. Be sure to discern who you can open your heart and life to. God has ordained certain relationships in your life. Those relationships should enhance the quality of your life and take you to a higher level. They should inspire you to go further than you ever imagined.

So before you open your mouth, be sure to ask yourself "Is this *really* worth saying or should I just keep my peace?"

The Fortune Cookie

I have a confession. I'm addicted to Asian food! Always have been. If given a choice of a hamburger or a stir-fry dish, I'm going with the stir-fry 99% of the time. I don't know exactly when my love affair began with Asian food, but it is a part of who I am. I have come to accept that. I recall one particular trip to one of my favorite restaurants and an experience with a traditional Chinese "dessert" – the fortune cookie. When I opened my cookie, it contained a simple yet profound message in it. It simply said:

"Work on improving your exercise routine."

At first glance, I thought to myself, "Yeah, I do need to get back in the gym and re-establish my exercise routine." But after a little more thought, the Lord began to minister to me and here is what He taught me. I believe that you will find this to be applicable to your life as well.

It's amazing what happens when you begin to slow down and break some things down. Here are the lessons:

1. **<u>Work</u>**. It's a simple principle but one that needs to be put into practice. We have to stay active and busy doing God's will for our lives. There are many people who desire certain things in their lives but they are not willing to work for them. Jesus taught us to "occupy until He comes." Take the time to work on your vision. Work on your dream. Work on accomplishing your goals.

2. **<u>Work on</u>**. There are many people who work IN certain things but very few work ON. A lot of people work IN their marriages, but few people work ON their marriages. Many people work IN a particular profession, but few take the time to work ON themselves. It's amazing what can happen when you simply focus on working ON various things.

3. **<u>Work on improving</u>**. The process of life is to evaluate, adjust, and improve. Based

on that principle, improvement can only come as a result of first evaluating where you are and then making the necessary adjustments. As a person of excellence, you should always strive to work on improving – yourself, your relationship with God, your prayer life, your skill set, your relationships, and your knowledge base.

4. **Exercise**. You will never reach your full potential without exercise – physically or spiritually. That is why it is critical to exercise. Physically, you must exercise your heart and your mind. Spiritually, you must exercise your faith. The benefits of exercise are absolutely awesome. Physically, you have more energy. You maintain your ideal weight and size. And you often experience less stress. Spiritually, God will give you more energy. He will allow you to carry more "weight." And He will allow you to eliminate stress by allowing you to place your burdens upon Him.

5. **Routine**. Practice doesn't make perfect,

but it certainly makes better. Developing a routine helps you to have consistency with your desired results. Routine also eliminates the need for you to think about recurring tasks or events in your life. Routine isn't always the most fun thing to set in order, but it certainly helps to make life easier. Setting a schedule, or routine, actually tells your time where to go instead of wondering where it went. Take the time to set routines in your life.

A very simple message from a very simple dessert. Never minimize a great message that may come in a small package.

What Next, Lord?

I am an extremely process-oriented, logical steps kinda guy.

Stop → Drop→Roll
Elementary school → Middle school → High school → College
Love → Marriage → Baby carriage (even though it doesn't happen like this much nowadays)

But I certainly believe in logical steps. In addition to that, I am the type of person who is NEVER satisfied with where I am. Maybe I should restate that. I am the type of person who is never complacent, but I am content. Although I am content with who I am and where God is taking me, I am constantly striving for something beyond where I currently am. I set loftier goals than I believe that I'm able to achieve in my own strength. I desire to strengthen my relationship with God more and more each day. I desire to love my wife and children more and more each day. I desire to learn something new every day that I can share with someone else. I never want to grow comfortable with "average" or "the status quo." That's not how I'm wired.

Not long ago, I had a few financial goals for myself that I accomplished. And while I did take the time to celebrate the achievement of those goals, my spirit immediately posed the question "What next, Lord?" Yes, I am overjoyed that I hit the goals that I set for myself, however, I realize that there is more to be done. More lives to be touched. More families to be impacted. More testimonies to be established. More people to set free.

As soon as I overcome one hurdle in my life, I'm constantly looking and asking "What next, Lord?" Even though we all experience various trials and difficulties, we must find the strength to ask "What next, Lord?" I'm a firm believer that God never ends on a negative. So if you are experiencing negativity in your life right now, you can rest assured that it's not the end. God has your best interest at heart and desires for you to be the best you that you can possibly be.

I encourage you to take the time to get quiet and sincerely ask God "What next, Lord?" Often times, we are so busy with things that we don't take the time to reflect on our experiences and process what has happened to us. Ask yourself "What next, Lord? Who are you helping me to become? What are you calling me to do? What do you desire for me to have? What next, Lord?"

If you desire to grow to a new level in your life, you must:
1. Ask the right questions.
2. Ask the right questions to the right people.
3. Act at the right time.

Keep your eyes and ears open to the next thing that God has in store for you!

Jason H. Thomas

Closing Thoughts

The greatest thing about the gift of encouragement is that it is absolutely free. It doesn't cost you anything to encourage someone else by offering a smile or kind word. In addition, it is rare that your joy and peace is diminished after you encourage another person. As a matter of fact, the opposite is usually true. Often times, you will walk away feeling fulfilled and energized after you've taken the time to encourage someone else. Encouragement is one of the greatest gifts that we can give to others.

Encouragement is also contagious and very addictive. Whenever you encourage a person, something in you should yearn to look for opportunities to encourage other people. Elizabeth Harrison stated it best when she said "Those who are lifting the world upward and onward are those who encourage more than criticize." We must be committed to constantly encouraging the people around us. Encouragement eliminates excuses, removes barriers, expands potential, provides perspective, and unleashes passion.

My desire is that you walk away from reading this book as a person who is committed to becoming an encourager on a daily basis. It's been said that people have a greater need to be reminded than they do to be informed. In other words, people need encouragement more than anything else. Often times, people know WHAT to do. They just need someone to serve as the wind beneath their wings.

Sidney Madwed said "The finest gift you can give anyone is encouragement. Yet, almost no one gets the encouragement they need to grow to their full potential. If everyone received the encouragement they need to grow, the genius in most everyone would blossom and the world would produce abundance beyond the wildest dreams." Take the time to encourage someone today and unlock their potential so that the world can benefit from what they have to offer.

Acknowledgements

I am who I am because of my Lord and Savior, Jesus Christ, and the people that God has brought into my life. This book is the result of the love, prayers, and encouragement of many people.

Thank you to all my family, friends, and loved ones who believed in me and encouraged me to take risks, to live a life pleasing unto God, and to leave a lasting legacy. Mom, thank you for being who you are – selfless and supportive. Your servant's heart and compassion for people is now a defining characteristic of my life. Dad, thank you for showing me what it means to be a man and teaching me how to appreciate life. I am proud to be your son and grateful to be your friend. Bernard and Linda, thank you for being the best brother and sister that I could've ever asked for. Breland, Lauryn, Bryton, and Lindsey, know that your Uncle J loves you more than you can fathom. I believe in your God-given destinies and will continue to support you any ways that I can. Godmommie, thank you for teaching me what it truly means to trust God. I love you and appreciate you! To my grandparents who have already transitioned to heaven – T. Herman Graves, Jr., Mildred Graves, and Henrietta Rogers – thank you for EVERYTHING. Your seed remains in the earth and is bearing fruit that shall remain. To my DC family, thanks for allowing me to be me and loving me still.

Thank you to the faith families and communities who have helped to shape my core belief system – Word of Faith Family Worship Cathedral, Word of Faith Love Center, First Congregational Church, Ark of Salvation, Community of Faith Family Church, Holy Temple Church of Christ, Impact Church, The Courageous Church.

Thank you to the teachers and professors who have fostered in me a lifelong love and appreciation for learning – Peyton Forest Elementary School, Southwest Middle School,

Frederick Douglass High School, The Paideia School, Washington University in St. Louis, Christian Life School of Theology.

Thank you to my spiritual father and mentor, Bishop Dale C. Bronner. What can I say to truly express my gratitude? I appreciate you setting a consistent example for me to follow. God couldn't have blessed me with a greater "faith general" to have relationship with. I love you!

Thank you to my Peter, James, and John – Michael D. Polk, Lorenzo D. King, and Marquis L. Phelps. Thank you for teaching me the true meaning of friendship. I love y'all and appreciate you more than you know.

Thank you to my mentors and friends – Reginald and Lisa Garmon, John and Johnetta Williams, Dwight and Desiree Andrews, Michael and Linda Chinn, George and Yvonne Amos, Charles and Alisa Battle, Alvin Hobbs, Charles Houston, C. Elijah Bronner, Olu Brown, Shaun King, Jose Adames, Sabrina

Stewart, Marian Barnes, Tolton Pace, Eugene Hillsman, Ryonnel Jackson, Jerome Strickland, Jr., Windsor Williams, III.

Thank you to my firstborn son, Jonathan David. You have changed my life and motivated me more than you will ever know. I love your energy, passion, and zeal for life. You are destined for greatness and will do great things for the Kingdom of God! I believe in your destiny and promise to do my part to introduce you to the person who will help you more than I ever could – Jesus Christ.

Last but certainly not least, I want to thank my helpmeet, my gift from God, my "good thing", my best friend, Pearilya LaRae Thomas. Your love has meant more to me than you'll ever know! Your faith in me keeps me going even when I feel like giving up! Your hope inspires me to be better and do better! You are a phenomenal wife and an exceptional mother to Jonathan (and our future children). My life is more fulfilling because you are a part of it.

For all that you do and all that you are, thank you.

For more information on products and resources or if you'd like to send comments or feedback, contact Jason via email at jason.h.thomas@ hotmail.com.